Bless My ~~Family~~

Photographed and hand painted by Kathleen Francour
Stories by Sylvia Seymour

Photography © 1997 Kathleen Francour
Carefree, Arizona. All rights reserved.

ISBN: 0-7853-2120-9

Jesus Loves
the
Little Children

PUBLICATIONS INTERNATIONAL, LTD.
7373 North Cicero Avenue
Lincolnwood, Illinois 60646

A Real Family

"One, two, three, four, five, six," Jason counted the people in the book that he was reading. "This family has six people."

"That's a big family," said Mother.

"One, two, three, four, five: That's another big family."

Dad was reading the newspaper, but he stopped and motioned to Jason to come sit on his lap.

"Dad," asked Jason, "why don't WE have a big family? There are only three of us. Are we a REAL family?"

"Jason," said Dad, "it doesn't matter how many people are in a family. It's the love that the family has for each other that makes it a REAL family."

I sought my soul,
    But my soul I could not see.
I sought my God,
    But my God eluded me.
I sought my brother,
    And found all three.

Honor your father and your mother.

Exodus 20:1

Lord Jesus,
Please take care of my family.
Keep them healthy and safe from harm.
I love them very much.

                                              Amen.

Dear Jesus,
My parents work very hard
to bring me the things I need.
Please help me to be good
so that their lives are a little easier.
Thank you, Lord.

                                              Amen.

Who Wants to Play with a Sister

"Mommy, why can't Billy and Tommy come over?" whined Daniel. "I want to play with them. They are my best friends."

"Why don't you play with Kimberly?"

"Kimberly's my sister! Who wants to play with a little sister!"

Kimberly came into the room carrying two cowboy hats. "Hi, Daniel. Let's play cowboy. I have some hats. We can use broomsticks for horses."

The children asked their mom for two brooms. "Yahoo!" cheered Kimberly.

"Let's go outside and ride our horses," said Daniel.

"Good idea, big brother," said Kimberly.

"Hey, this is fun! I'm glad you're my sister."

I know that as I grow bigger
my love for my mother and father
will grow bigger, too.
Thank you, Jesus, for my parents.

Dear Lord,
Thank you for my grandparents.
They always have time to read to me
or play games.
They like to tickle and play and laugh.
And they like ice cream
and going to the park, too.
Mostly though, God, they love me.
Please take care of them, Lord,
I think they must be a lot like You.

Thank you, Lord Jesus,
for my brothers and sisters.
Without them, our house
would be too quiet.

Dear Jesus,
My brother and I may
sometimes fight, but I know
that he loves me and I love him.
Please know, Lord Jesus,
that we love You, too.

Family Pictures

Mathew looked at the picture he had drawn of Mommy, Daddy, brother Aaron, baby Lauren, and Whiskers.

"It doesn't look right. No one looks right. I just can't draw." Tears trickled down Mathew's cheeks. He wanted to tear up the picture and throw it away.

"Let me see your picture," said Aaron. He looked carefully at the picture his brother had made.
"Why this is beautiful, Mathew. I like the way you put a smile on each of our faces. Jesus thinks that children's pictures are the best kind, especially pictures of happy smiling faces."

Then Mathew smiled!

Here on my bed my limbs I lay,
    God grant me grace my prayers to say:
O God! preserve my mother dear
    In strength and health for many a year;
And, O preserve my father, too,
    And may I pay him reverence due;
And may I my best thoughts employ
    To be my parents' hope and joy;
And, O preserve my brothers both
    From evil doings and from sloth,
And may we always love each other,
    Our friends, our father, and our mother:
And still, O Lord, to me impart
    An innocent and grateful heart,
That after my great sleep I may
    Awake to Thy eternal day! Amen.

Samuel Taylor Coleridge

Peace be to this house
and to all who dwell in it.
Peace be to them that enter
and to them that depart.

Dear Lord,
Please be sure that my family
knows that I love them very much,
even during the times I don't show it.

Amen.

God bless all those that I love.

God bless all those that love me.

God bless all those that love those that I love,

And all those that love those who love me.